The Resilient Manager: How to Bounce Back from Setbacks and Thrive in Adversity

Iqbal Shah

DEDICATION

This book is dedicated to my beloved brothers, Sharif Khan and Israr Khan. Throughout my journey, they have been my pillars of strength, providing unwavering support and encouragement. Their belief in my abilities and their constant words of encouragement have fueled my determination to bring this book to fruition. Sharif and Israr, thank you for being my guiding lights and for always inspiring me to reach for the stars.

I would also like to dedicate this book to my dear friends, Akbar Shah and Falak Niaz. Their presence in my life has been invaluable, and their friendship has been a constant source of inspiration. Their thoughtful feedback and critical analysis have played a significant role in shaping this book, pushing me to refine my ideas and present them in the best possible way. Akbar and Falak, thank you for your unwavering support and for being my sounding boards throughout this journey.

Furthermore, I dedicate this book to my nephews, Farman Khan and Shahzain Khan. Their innocent smiles and boundless energy bring immeasurable joy to my life. Their presence has been a source of inspiration and motivation throughout the writing process. Farman and Shahzain, thank you for filling my days with laughter and reminding me of the importance of embracing joy and simplicity.

To my brothers, friends, and nephews, your love, support, and encouragement have been the driving force behind this book. You have believed in me, cheered me on during moments of doubt, and celebrated my achievements. This book is a testament to the strength of our bonds and the impact you have had on my life. May this dedication serve as a token of my deep gratitude and appreciation for your presence in my journey.

I offer this book to you, hoping that it will inspire and empower you in your own endeavors. May it serve as a reminder that with dedication, perseverance, and the support of loved ones, we can overcome any obstacles and make a meaningful difference in the world. Thank you for being a part of my life and for being the driving force behind my pursuit of knowledge and growth.

CONTENTS

ACKNOWLEDGMENTS

I would like to express my heartfelt gratitude to my brothers, Sharif Khan and Israr Khan, for their unwavering support and encouragement throughout this book's journey. Your belief in my abilities and constant motivation have been instrumental in bringing this project to fruition. Your guidance and wise counsel have helped shape my ideas, and I am forever grateful for the love and support you have shown me.

I extend my deepest appreciation to my dear friends, Akbar Shah and Falak Niaz, for their invaluable contributions to this book. Your positive feedback, critical analysis, and thought-provoking discussions have played a significant role in refining the concepts and enhancing the overall quality of this work. Your friendship and intellectual companionship have been a constant source of inspiration, and I am privileged to have you in my life.

To my nephews, Farman Khan and Shahzain Khan, I want to express my heartfelt thanks for being a source of joy and inspiration. Your innocence, laughter, and boundless energy have provided a much-needed respite during the challenging moments of writing. Your presence in my life has reminded me of the importance of embracing simplicity and finding happiness in the little things. Thank you for being my constant reminders of the beauty of life.

I would also like to extend my gratitude to all the individuals who have supported me throughout this book's creation. To my mentors, whose guidance and expertise have shaped my understanding and approach, I am truly grateful. To the research participants and case study organizations who generously shared their experiences and insights, thank you for providing real-world examples that enriched the content.

My appreciation extends to the team at the publishing house for their dedication, professionalism, and commitment to bringing this book to life. Your expertise and support have been invaluable in transforming the manuscript into a finished product that I am proud to share with the world.

Last but not least, I would like to express my deepest gratitude to my readers. Your interest in this book and your commitment to making a difference in the non-profit sector inspire me. I hope that the knowledge and strategies shared in these pages empower you to create positive change and foster financial sustainability in your organizations.

In conclusion, I am humbled and grateful for the support and encouragement I have received from my brothers, friends, nephews, mentors, and the publishing team. Without your unwavering belief in me and your contributions, this book would not have been possible. Thank you for being an integral part of this journey and for your continued support in my pursuit of making a meaningful impact in the non-profit sector.

Preface

In today's dynamic and rapidly changing business landscape, the role of a manager has evolved beyond traditional responsibilities. The modern manager is not only tasked with driving results and overseeing teams but also with navigating a complex web of challenges, uncertainties, and setbacks. As organizations face unprecedented disruptions, it is imperative for managers to possess a unique set of skills that go beyond technical expertise and delve into the realm of resilience.

"The Resilient Manager: How to Bounce Back from Setbacks and Thrive in Adversity" is a guide crafted to equip managers with the essential toolkit needed to not only survive but thrive in the face of adversity. This book is not just about surviving the storm, but emerging from it stronger, more adaptable, and better prepared for the future.

Resilience, in the context of managerial roles, encompasses a spectrum of skills and qualities that empower leaders to respond effectively to unexpected challenges. From adapting to change and overcoming setbacks to fostering resilient teams and leading through adversity, each chapter of this book delves into key aspects of building and sustaining resilience in a managerial role.

Drawing from real-world examples, case studies, and insights from diverse industries, "The Resilient Manager" takes a holistic approach to resilience. It examines the critical role of mindset, communication, innovation, self-care, and leadership in cultivating resilience not just for the manager, but for the entire team.

This book does not just provide a theoretical framework but offers actionable strategies, practical tips, and guidelines that can be immediately applied in the real world. It aims to guide managers in fostering a culture of resilience within their teams and organizations, driving not only individual success but also organizational growth.

As you embark on this journey through the pages of "The Resilient Manager," prepare to uncover the power of resilience and its transformative impact on your managerial style. Embrace the stories of those who have navigated challenges, harnessed setbacks as opportunities, and emerged as stronger leaders. This book is an invitation to explore the potential within yourself, to adapt, innovate, and lead with grace through the inevitable storms of professional life.

Whether you're a seasoned manager seeking to enhance your leadership skills or an aspiring leader looking to develop a foundation of resilience, this book offers insights that transcend industries and roles. The journey of resilience is not without its challenges, but it is a journey that promises growth, empowerment, and a lasting legacy of impactful leadership.

Introduction

In the dynamic and unpredictable landscape of business and leadership, the ability to bounce back from setbacks and thrive amidst adversity is a defining trait of successful managers. Welcome to "The Resilient Manager: How to Bounce Back from Setbacks and Thrive in Adversity." This book is a comprehensive guide that delves into the core principles, strategies, and practices that empower managers to cultivate resilience within themselves and their teams.

In an era where change is the only constant and disruptions are commonplace, resilience has emerged as a crucial skill for effective leadership. This book is designed to be your roadmap to mastering this essential trait. Each chapter is carefully curated to provide insights, actionable steps, and real-world examples that illuminate the path towards becoming a resilient manager.

From the outset, we will explore the concept of resilience, dissecting its multifaceted dimensions and understanding its relevance in the context of modern management. The journey continues as we dive into the crucial role of mindset, discovering how the way you perceive challenges and setbacks shapes your ability to overcome them. Through case studies and practical advice, we will uncover the strategies that empower managers to adapt, innovate, and lead with confidence.

Communication, a cornerstone of effective leadership, takes center stage as we examine how resilient managers harness the power of transparent and empathetic communication to foster trust, collaboration, and cohesion within their teams. But resilience goes beyond mere communication; it extends into creating a culture of innovation, where adversity becomes a catalyst for creativity and growth.

The book also delves into the often overlooked aspect of self-care. As a resilient manager, it's imperative to not only lead others but to prioritize your own well-being. We will explore techniques to manage stress, maintain work-life balance, and develop emotional intelligence – all integral to sustaining resilience over the long haul.

In leadership, adaptability and preparedness are paramount. The chapters on leading through adversity and crisis management provide invaluable guidance on steering teams through tumultuous times while maintaining focus on the larger mission. Real-world case studies will illustrate the application of these strategies in different organizational contexts.

From practical tips for fostering resilient teams to insights on maintaining ethical standards in challenging situations, "The Resilient Manager" is a comprehensive resource that covers every facet of resilience in managerial roles. Each chapter is not just a theoretical exploration but a practical toolkit, offering actionable steps and guidelines that you can implement immediately to enhance your resilience as a manager.

Throughout the book, you will find stories of managers who turned setbacks into stepping stones, transformed challenges into opportunities, and emerged as stronger, more impactful leaders. As you read on, consider this book as a mentor, guiding you through the intricacies of developing resilience – a skill that not only defines your success as a manager but also leaves a lasting legacy of leadership excellence.

So, embark on this transformative journey as we explore what it takes to become a truly resilient manager – one who not only navigates adversity but emerges as a beacon of strength, adaptability, and inspiration for their teams and organizations. The path to resilience begins here, and your journey to becoming "The Resilient Manager" starts now.

Chapter 1

Understanding Resilience

Understanding Resilience: Navigating Challenges and Thriving in Adversity

Resilience, in its essence, is the remarkable ability of individuals, communities, and even entire societies to adapt, bounce back, and thrive in the face of adversity, setbacks, and challenges. It's the strength to withstand difficult circumstances, recover from hardships, and continue progressing toward personal and collective goals. Resilience is not merely about surviving; it's about thriving despite the odds, emerging stronger, and using adversity as a catalyst for growth and positive transformation.

Components of Resilience

- Adaptability: Resilient individuals are flexible and open to change. They adjust their mindset and strategies when faced with unexpected circumstances, demonstrating a willingness to embrace new ways of thinking and doing.

- Emotional Regulation: Resilience involves managing emotions effectively. Individuals with strong resilience can acknowledge their feelings, express them constructively, and regain emotional balance even in challenging situations.

- Problem-Solving: Resilience requires a proactive approach to problem-solving. Rather than being overwhelmed by difficulties, resilient individuals analyze challenges, break them down into manageable steps, and seek viable solutions.

- Social Support: Building a network of relationships is vital for resilience. Having a support system—friends, family, mentors—offers emotional validation, advice, and encouragement during tough times.

- Positive Mindset: Resilient individuals maintain a positive outlook. They focus on opportunities, personal strengths, and past successes, allowing them to face adversity with hope and determination.

- Self-Care: Prioritizing self-care is essential. Resilient individuals recognize the importance of physical, mental, and emotional well-being, adopting practices that recharge their energy.

- Coping Strategies: Resilience involves having healthy coping mechanisms. Engaging in activities like exercise, meditation, journaling, or creative pursuits helps manage stress and foster resilience.

Building Resilience

- Developing Self-Awareness: Understand your strengths, weaknesses, and triggers. Self-awareness enables you to recognize your emotional responses and empowers you to manage them effectively.

- Cultivating Positivity: Focus on gratitude, optimism, and cultivating a positive outlook. Challenge negative thought patterns and practice reframing difficulties as opportunities for growth.

- Setting Realistic Goals: Break down larger goals into smaller, achievable steps. Success in these micro-goals reinforces a sense of accomplishment and contributes to overall resilience.

- Fostering Connections: Build a support network of people who uplift you. Healthy relationships provide emotional validation and serve as a buffer during tough times.

- Practicing Self-Care: Prioritize activities that nourish your well-being—exercise, restful sleep, a balanced diet, hobbies, and spending time in nature.

- Strengthening Problem-Solving Skills: Develop your ability to identify challenges, analyze potential solutions, and make informed decisions. Problem-solving is a cornerstone of resilience.

- Adapting to Change: Embrace change as a natural part of life. Viewing change as an opportunity for growth rather than a threat enhances your resilience.

- Learning from Setbacks: Rather than dwelling on failures, extract lessons from setbacks. Every challenge offers an opportunity to learn, adapt, and improve.

The Role of Resilience in Different Contexts

- Personal Resilience: In your personal life, resilience helps you navigate personal losses, relationship difficulties, and health challenges. It empowers you to bounce back from setbacks, fostering mental and emotional well-being.

- Professional Resilience: In the workplace, resilience enables you to handle work-related stress, setbacks, and changes. Resilient professionals are adaptable, maintain productivity, and exhibit leadership qualities.

- Community Resilience: Communities with strong resilience effectively recover from disasters, economic downturns, and social challenges. They come together, support each other, and work collaboratively to rebuild and improve.

- Global Resilience: On a global scale, resilience is crucial for addressing complex challenges such as climate change, pandemics, and geopolitical tensions. Countries and international organizations need to collaborate and adapt to ensure a sustainable future.

The Benefits of Resilience

- Enhanced Mental Health: Resilience promotes psychological well-being by reducing stress, anxiety, and depression. It enables individuals to handle adversity without being overwhelmed.

- Improved Problem-Solving: Resilient individuals approach

challenges with a problem-solving mindset, allowing them to find effective solutions and make informed decisions.

- Better Relationships: Strong resilience fosters healthier relationships. The ability to manage emotions and communicate effectively contributes to positive interactions.

- Increased Productivity: Resilient individuals remain productive even in difficult circumstances. They adapt to changes, maintain focus, and contribute effectively to their tasks and responsibilities.

- Personal Growth: Adversity fosters personal growth. Resilient individuals learn from their experiences, develop new skills, and gain a deeper understanding of themselves.

Resilience is an invaluable skill that empowers individuals, communities, and societies to navigate the complexities of life with strength and grace. It's not about avoiding challenges but about developing the tools to face them head-on. Through self-awareness, positivity, problem-solving, and strong connections, anyone can cultivate resilience and emerge from adversity as a stronger, more adaptable, and empowered individual.

Definition of Resilience in a Managerial Context

Resilience in a managerial context is characterized by the ability of leaders to adapt, recover, and flourish in the midst of adversity, uncertainty, and challenging situations within the organizational landscape. This form of resilience extends beyond personal fortitude; it involves the skillful management of resources, people, and strategies to ensure the continued progress and success of the team and the organization as a whole.

Key Elements of Managerial Resilience

- Adaptive Leadership: Resilient managers possess the capability to adjust their leadership style and strategies to align with changing circumstances. They remain agile in their approach, shifting priorities as needed while maintaining a clear vision.

- Decision-Making Under Pressure: Managerial resilience requires the capacity to make well-informed decisions even in high-pressure scenarios. Resilient managers maintain a rational mindset, analyze available information, and choose the most suitable course of action.

- Crisis Management: Resilient managers excel in crisis management. They remain composed when facing critical situations, demonstrating the ability to prioritize tasks, delegate responsibilities, and provide guidance to their team during turbulent times.

- Resource Optimization: Effectively utilizing resources is a hallmark of managerial resilience. Resilient managers allocate resources efficiently, adapting budgets, manpower, and assets to address unforeseen challenges without compromising overall objectives.

- Change Navigation: Organizations are subject to constant change. Resilient managers guide their teams through transformations, ensuring that the workforce remains motivated, engaged, and productive even during periods of uncertainty.

- Team Empowerment: Resilient managers empower their teams by fostering an environment of trust, open communication, and collaboration. This empowers employees to contribute their insights and skills, enhancing the overall resilience of the organization.

- Learning from Setbacks: Managerial resilience involves learning from failures and setbacks. Rather than dwelling on mistakes, resilient managers facilitate post-event analysis to extract lessons that can inform future strategies.

- Vision and Adaptation: While resilience entails dealing with challenges, it also involves maintaining a long-term vision. Resilient managers continuously adapt their strategies to ensure alignment with organizational goals, despite external disruptions.

Why Managerial Resilience Matters

- Organizational Stability: Resilient managers contribute to the stability and continuity of an organization, even during turbulent times. Their ability to lead effectively ensures that operations continue with minimal disruptions.

- Employee Morale: A resilient manager inspires confidence and trust among team members. Their unwavering demeanor and skilled navigation of challenges create a positive work environment and boost employee morale.

- Innovation and Growth: Resilient managers foster an environment where innovation and creativity thrive. They encourage employees to explore new approaches and solutions, even when faced with obstacles.

- Effective Change Management: As organizations evolve, resilience enables managers to lead successful change initiatives. Resilient leaders can communicate changes effectively, mitigate resistance, and guide the workforce through transitions.

- Adaptation to Market Shifts: Markets are dynamic, and resilience enables managers to adapt swiftly to shifting trends, technological advancements, and competitive pressures.

Cultivating Managerial Resilience

- Continuous Learning: Managers should engage in ongoing learning to stay updated with the latest industry trends, management techniques, and crisis management strategies.

- Mentorship and Coaching: Seeking guidance from experienced mentors and coaches provides valuable insights and perspectives that can enhance resilience.

- Building Emotional Intelligence: Emotional intelligence is essential for managerial resilience. Understanding and managing one's own emotions and empathizing with others contribute to effective leadership during challenges.

- Scenario Planning: Developing contingency plans for various scenarios helps managers respond quickly and strategically to unforeseen events.

- Self-Care: A key aspect of resilience is taking care of one's physical and mental well-being. Managers who prioritize self-care are better equipped to handle stress and maintain their resilience.

Managerial resilience is a multifaceted trait that empowers leaders to navigate the complexities of the business world with adaptability, composure, and effectiveness. Resilient managers inspire their teams, drive innovation, and ensure organizational success, even in the face of adversity. By continuously honing their skills, fostering a supportive work environment, and embracing change as an opportunity, resilient managers play a pivotal role in guiding their organizations toward growth, stability, and prosperity.

Importance of Resilience for Personal and Team Success

Resilience is integral for personal and team success as it empowers managers to remain composed and focused in high-pressure situations. It enables them to guide their teams through turbulent times, inspiring confidence and maintaining productivity. Resilient managers not only overcome setbacks themselves but also foster a resilient culture that permeates their teams.

Role of Mindset in Developing Resilience

A growth-oriented mindset is pivotal in developing resilience. Embracing challenges as opportunities for learning, reframing failures as stepping stones, and believing in one's ability to adapt and grow are central tenets of this mindset. The way managers perceive and approach challenges significantly influences their capacity to bounce back from setbacks.

Case Study: Non-profit Leader Adapting to Unexpected Funding Cuts

In a non-profit scenario, a leader faced unexpected funding cuts due to economic downturn. By leveraging a growth-oriented mindset, the leader reframed the situation as a chance to diversify funding sources. They rallied their team, fostering open communication, creative problem-solving, and collaborative brainstorming. This approach not only saved critical programs but also forged a stronger team bond.

Key Principles of Building Resilience in a Management Role

- Adaptability: Cultivate the ability to pivot and adjust strategies in response to changing circumstances.
- Emotional Intelligence: Enhance self-awareness and empathy to navigate interpersonal dynamics effectively.
- Stress Management: Develop coping mechanisms to handle stress and pressure while maintaining focus.
- Problem Solving: Strengthen analytical and critical thinking skills to tackle challenges systematically.
- Effective Communication: Foster transparent and open communication to maintain team cohesion.
- Self-Care: Prioritize self-care to sustain energy and well-being during demanding periods.
- Flexibility: Embrace change and uncertainty as opportunities for growth rather than threats.
- Learning Mindset: View failures as learning experiences and catalysts for improvement.
- Resilient Networking: Build a support network of mentors and peers to exchange insights and strategies.
- Strategic Planning: Develop contingency plans to anticipate potential setbacks and have proactive solutions in place.

Tips for Recognizing Signs of Burnout and Stress

- Change in Behavior: Observe shifts in behavior, such as decreased engagement or increased irritability.

- Physical Symptoms: Be attentive to physical signs like fatigue, sleep disturbances, or headaches.

- Reduced Performance: Notice declines in work quality, missed deadlines, or decreased productivity.

- Emotional Indicators: Pay attention to signs of emotional exhaustion, including mood swings or apathy.

- Isolation: If someone becomes increasingly withdrawn or avoids interactions, it might indicate burnout.

Setting Realistic Expectations for Yourself and Your Team

Setting realistic expectations involves aligning goals with available resources and timeframes. Acknowledge limitations and communicate transparently with your team about project scopes, potential challenges, and feasible outcomes. By fostering an environment of authenticity, you reduce undue pressure and set the stage for more achievable goals.

Techniques for Cultivating a Growth-Oriented Mindset

- Positive Self-Talk: Replace negative self-talk with affirmations that reinforce your ability to overcome challenges.

- Embrace Failure: View failures as stepping stones toward growth and opportunities for improvement.

- Continuous Learning: Seek opportunities for learning and skill development to enhance your capabilities.

- Seek Feedback: Embrace constructive feedback as a means to refine your skills and enhance performance.

- Focus on Solutions: Shift your focus from problems to solutions, encouraging proactive problem-solving.

Guidelines for Seeking Support and Mentorship

- Identify Mentors: Identify experienced individuals whose insights align with your goals and values.

- Open Communication: Approach mentors with a clear idea of what you seek and maintain open communication.

- Reciprocal Value: Ensure that the mentorship relationship is mutually beneficial, fostering a genuine exchange of knowledge and experience.

Incorporating Resilience as a Core Leadership Skill: Navigating Challenges with Strength and Grace

In a rapidly changing and unpredictable business landscape, resilience has emerged as a critical core leadership skill. Resilient leaders possess the ability to steer their teams through adversity, setbacks, and uncertainties while maintaining composure, adapting strategies, and fostering growth. This comprehensive exploration delves into the significance of incorporating resilience as a core leadership skill, offering examples, case studies, and practical insights.

· Understanding Resilience in Leadership

Resilience in leadership goes beyond personal fortitude; it involves the adept management of teams, resources, and strategies in the face of challenges. Resilient leaders inspire confidence and trust, making them adept at guiding their teams through turbulent waters while driving innovation and sustaining success.

Examples of Resilient Leadership

- Nelson Mandela: A prime example of resilience, Mandela endured 27 years in prison, emerging with an unwavering commitment to reconciliation and leadership. His ability to transform adversity into a unifying force showcased the power of resilience.

- Sheryl Sandberg: After the sudden loss of her husband, Sandberg, COO of Facebook, channeled her personal tragedy into a platform for discussing resilience. Her openness and determination in coping with grief exemplify resilient leadership.

Case Studies in Resilient Leadership

- Apple under Steve Jobs: Steve Jobs demonstrated resilience by leading Apple through multiple challenges, including product failures and internal conflicts. His unyielding vision and strategic shifts eventually transformed Apple into one of the most successful tech companies globally.

- IBM's Transformation: In the 1990s, IBM faced near-collapse due to changing market dynamics. CEO Lou Gerstner displayed resilience by making bold decisions to restructure the company, shift its focus, and revitalize its culture.

Benefits of Resilient Leadership

- Team Morale and Engagement: Resilient leaders create a positive work environment that supports employees during challenging times, boosting morale and engagement.

- Effective Crisis Management: Resilient leaders excel in crisis situations. Their ability to make informed decisions under pressure mitigates panic and guides the team toward solutions.

- Innovation and Adaptation: Resilient leaders foster a culture of innovation, encouraging team members to explore new approaches and adapt to changing circumstances.

- Change Management: Leaders with resilience navigate change effectively, ensuring that the team remains aligned, motivated, and productive during transitions.

Incorporating Resilience as a Core Skill

- Embrace Vulnerability: Resilient leaders are willing to show vulnerability and admit when challenges arise. This openness fosters trust and encourages collaboration.

- Build a Support Network: Cultivate a network of mentors, peers, and advisors who can provide guidance and insights during challenging times.

- Cultivate Emotional Intelligence: Developing emotional intelligence allows leaders to understand and manage their emotions while empathizing with others' perspectives.

- Promote Psychological Safety: A resilient leader ensures a psychologically safe environment where team members feel comfortable sharing concerns and challenges.

Practical Strategies for Resilient Leadership

- Scenario Planning: Anticipate potential challenges and develop contingency plans to navigate them effectively.

- Transparent Communication: Keep the team informed about developments, challenges, and the organization's approach to overcoming obstacles.

- Learning from Setbacks: Analyze failures and setbacks to extract lessons that can inform future strategies and decision-making.

- Encourage Continuous Learning: Resilient leaders value ongoing learning and professional development to stay adaptable in a rapidly changing world.

Incorporating resilience as a core leadership skill is paramount in today's dynamic business environment. Resilient leaders not only navigate challenges with grace but also empower their teams to thrive amidst adversity. Examples from iconic leaders and case studies illustrate how resilience can transform setbacks into stepping stones. By embracing vulnerability, building support networks, and promoting emotional intelligence, leaders can cultivate the resilience needed to steer their teams toward success, no matter the challenges that arise.

Chapter 2:

Adapting to Change

Change is an inevitable and constant force in the business landscape. In this chapter, we will explore the importance of embracing change, strategies for managing resistance within a team, a case study of successful team leadership during a rebranding process, and insights into identifying opportunities within challenges. We will also delve into navigating uncertainty with resilience, maintaining focus during transitions, effective leadership communication, fostering flexibility and creativity, building an adaptable culture, and finding the delicate balance between stability and innovation.

Embracing Change as a Constant in the Business Landscape

- **Change as the New Normal**: Acknowledge that change is a perpetual force in the business world and adaptability is a crucial skill for success.
- **Learning Mindset**: Embrace a learning-oriented mindset, treating change as an opportunity for growth and improvement.
- **Agility:** Develop organizational agility by being responsive to market shifts and customer preferences.
- **Innovation**: Use change as a catalyst for innovation, exploring new ideas and approaches to stay competitive.
- **Continuous Improvement**: View change as a chance to refine processes and strategies for enhanced efficiency.

Strategies for Managing Resistance to Change within a Team

- Effective Communication: Clearly communicate the reasons for the change, addressing any concerns and emphasizing the benefits.

- Involvement and Ownership: Involve team members in decision-making, empowering them to take ownership of the change process.

- Open Dialogue: Create a safe space for team members to voice their concerns and ask questions about the upcoming changes.

- Training and Support: Provide necessary training and support to ensure that team members are equipped to navigate the changes.

- Leading by Example: Demonstrate your own willingness to embrace change, setting a positive tone for the team.

Case Study: Leading Through a Rebranding Process

A retail manager successfully led their team through a rebranding process, offering valuable lessons in change management:

Background: The retail company decided to rebrand its image to align with evolving customer preferences.

- Clear Vision: The manager communicated a clear vision for the rebrand, explaining how it would benefit both the company and its customers.

- Empowerment: The team was empowered to contribute ideas and suggestions, fostering a sense of ownership.

- Open Communication: Regular meetings and updates kept the

team informed about the rebrand's progress, reducing uncertainty.

- Training and Transition: The manager organized training sessions to help team members adapt to new processes and technologies.
- Celebrating Milestones: Milestones achieved during the rebranding process were celebrated, boosting team morale.

Identifying Opportunities within Challenges

- Problem-Solving Mindset: Approach challenges as opportunities to find innovative solutions and improve processes.
- Market Insights: Use challenges as a way to gain deeper insights into customer needs and preferences.
- Skill Enhancement: Overcoming challenges often requires learning new skills, leading to personal and professional growth.
- Competitive Advantage: Successfully navigating challenges can lead to a competitive advantage in the long run.
- Collaboration: Challenges often require teamwork, fostering collaboration and stronger relationships within the team.

Navigating Uncertainty and Ambiguity with Resilience

- Adaptable Mindset: Cultivate adaptability by focusing on what you can control and remaining flexible in the face of uncertainty.
- Positive Attitude: Maintain a positive outlook, viewing uncertainties as opportunities to learn and grow.
- Stress Management: Develop stress management techniques to handle the pressures that come with uncertain situations.
- Problem Breakdown: Break down complex uncertainties into

smaller, manageable parts for easier decision-making.

- Continuous Learning: Use periods of uncertainty to expand your skill set and knowledge base, enhancing your value.

Tips for Maintaining Focus During Times of Change

- Set Clear Priorities: Define your priorities to stay focused on tasks that align with your goals.

- Time Management: Use effective time management techniques to allocate time for various tasks and minimize distractions.

- Mindfulness Practices: Incorporate mindfulness techniques to stay present and manage stress during times of change.

- Goal Visualization: Visualize the positive outcomes of the changes to maintain motivation and focus.

- Regular Check-Ins: Regularly assess your progress and adjust your focus based on changing circumstances.

Leading by Example and Communicating Change Effectively

- Authenticity: Be honest and transparent about the reasons for change, demonstrating authenticity as a leader.

- Two-Way Communication: Encourage open dialogue, listening to concerns and feedback from team members.

- Consistent Updates: Provide regular updates on the progress of changes, keeping the team informed and engaged.

- Empathy: Understand that team members might have different reactions to change and show empathy towards their feelings.

- Positive Language: Use positive language to convey the benefits of the change, inspiring optimism within the team.

Encouraging Flexibility and Creativity Among Team Members

- Supportive Environment: Create an environment where team members feel comfortable proposing creative solutions and trying new approaches.
- Diverse Perspectives: Encourage diverse viewpoints and ideas, fostering a culture of innovation.
- Freedom to Experiment: Allow team members the freedom to experiment with new ideas, even if they involve risks.
- Recognition: Recognize and reward creative thinking, motivating team members to continue seeking innovative solutions.
- Learning from Failure: Embrace failures as opportunities to learn and grow, encouraging a culture that values risk-taking.

Building a Culture That Values Adaptability

- Leadership Commitment: Leaders should demonstrate and emphasize the importance of adaptability through their actions.
- Continuous Learning: Promote a culture of continuous learning and skill development to enhance adaptability.
- Feedback Culture: Create an environment where giving and receiving constructive feedback is encouraged.
- Flexibility in Processes: Ensure that processes are flexible enough to accommodate changes and improvements.
- Celebrating Adaptability: Acknowledge and celebrate instances where team members demonstrated adaptability in challenging situations.

Balancing Stability with Innovation

- Stable Core Values: Maintain core values and principles while embracing innovative changes.

- Risk Assessment: Evaluate the potential risks and benefits of innovations before implementing them.

- Pilot Programs: Test new ideas on a smaller scale before rolling them out to the entire team or organization.

- Continuous Improvement: Combine stability with a commitment to continuously improve processes and approaches.

- Feedback Loop: Establish a feedback loop to monitor the impact of innovations and make necessary adjustments.

Adapting to change is a fundamental skill in the dynamic business landscape. Embracing change, managing resistance, and leading through uncertainties are key components of successful change management. By fostering creativity, flexibility, and an adaptable culture, organizations can not only navigate challenges but also identify opportunities for growth. Effective leadership communication, maintaining focus, and striking the right balance between stability and innovation are essential for achieving lasting success in times of change.

Chapter 3

Overcoming Setbacks

In the journey towards success, setbacks are inevitable. However, these setbacks can serve as valuable learning opportunities and catalysts for growth. In this chapter, we will explore how to view setbacks as stepping stones, techniques for reframing failures, a compelling case study of a startup founder's rebound, managing emotions, problem-solving strategies, maintaining team morale, and fostering accountability and growth in a blame-free environment. We'll also delve into guidelines for constructive post-setback analysis and building resilience through continuous improvement.

Viewing Setbacks as Learning Opportunities

- Shift in Perspective: Rather than seeing setbacks as failures, view them as opportunities to learn, adapt, and improve for the future.

- Growth Mindset: Embrace a growth mindset, where setbacks are seen as stepping stones towards personal and professional development.

- Identify Lessons: Analyze setbacks to identify lessons learned, allowing you to make informed decisions in the future.

Techniques for Reframing Failures into Stepping Stones

- Reframe with Positivity: Reframe failures as temporary setbacks on the path to success, focusing on the lessons gained.

- Challenge Assumptions: Question assumptions that may have led to the setback and explore alternative approaches.

- Visualize Success: Envision overcoming the setback and achieving success, reinforcing your determination to persevere.

Case Study: Startup Founder Rebounding from Product Launch Failure

In a remarkable case study, a determined startup founder faced a major setback when their highly anticipated product launch failed to gain traction. Rather than succumbing to defeat, the founder employed these strategies:

- Emotional Resilience: The founder acknowledged their emotions but quickly shifted focus towards solutions.

- Analyzing Failure: Thoroughly examined the reasons behind the product's failure, identifying gaps in market research and user feedback.

- Iterative Approach: Utilized the setback as an opportunity to iterate and refine the product, addressing the identified shortcomings.

- Engaging Team: Maintained open communication with the team, fostering a collaborative environment to brainstorm new strategies.

Managing Emotions and Maintaining Composure

- Acknowledge Emotions: Allow yourself to experience the emotions triggered by setbacks, but avoid dwelling on negativity.
- Time for Reflection: Take a brief pause to reflect before responding emotionally, ensuring a measured and composed reaction.
- Positive Self-Talk: Practice positive self-talk to reframe setbacks and maintain a constructive mindset.

Strategies for Problem-Solving and Resourcefulness

- Identify Root Causes: Dig deep to uncover the root causes of setbacks, enabling targeted solutions.
- Creative Solutions: Encourage brainstorming sessions to generate creative solutions that address the challenges faced.
- Resource Optimization: Utilize existing resources effectively, finding innovative ways to overcome obstacles with limited means.

Tips for Regaining Team Morale After Setbacks

- Transparent Communication: Share setbacks transparently with the team, fostering an environment of honesty and openness.
- Focus on Progress: Highlight the progress made despite setbacks, showcasing the team's resilience and determination.

- Celebrate Small Wins: Acknowledge and celebrate small victories along the way, boosting morale and motivation.

Accepting Responsibility and Taking Accountability

- Ownership of Mistakes: Embrace accountability for setbacks, demonstrating a commitment to rectify and learn from them.
- Lead by Example: Set an example by admitting your mistakes and showing that accountability is a value held by everyone.
- Collaborative Problem-Solving: Involve the team in finding solutions, promoting a collective responsibility for overcoming setbacks.

Fostering a Blame-Free Environment and Promoting Growth

- No-Blame Culture: Establish a culture where setbacks are not met with blame but are seen as opportunities for improvement.
- Constructive Feedback: Encourage feedback that focuses on solutions and improvement, rather than assigning blame.
- Individual Development: Support individual growth by offering resources and training to help team members overcome setbacks.

Guidelines for Constructive Post-Setback Analysis

- Objective Assessment: Evaluate setbacks objectively, focusing on facts rather than emotions.
- Identify Patterns: Look for recurring patterns in setbacks to address underlying issues systematically.
- Feedback Collection: Seek input from team members,

stakeholders, and external sources to gain diverse perspectives.

Building Resilience Through Continuous Improvement

- Adaptive Learning: Apply lessons from setbacks to adapt and refine strategies, contributing to continuous improvement.
- Resilience Training: Offer training and resources to team members to enhance their emotional resilience and coping skills.
- Celebrate Progress: Recognize and celebrate the progress made after setbacks, reinforcing the culture of growth and resilience.

Setbacks are not roadblocks, but opportunities for growth. By viewing setbacks through a positive lens, practicing emotional management, employing effective problem-solving strategies, and fostering a culture of accountability and growth, individuals and teams can overcome obstacles and emerge stronger than before. The case study of the startup founder's rebound serves as a testament to the transformative power of perseverance and strategic thinking. Ultimately, setbacks can become stepping stones on the journey to success, shaping resilient individuals and organizations.

Chapter 4

Leading Through Adversity

In the dynamic world of business, leaders face a multitude of challenges, especially during times of adversity. In this chapter, we will delve into the crucial role managers play in navigating challenging situations. We'll explore strategies for maintaining composure under pressure, fostering open communication, and making tough decisions while staying aligned with organizational values. Through a compelling case study, we'll witness a manager's journey through a company-wide restructuring. We'll also provide insights into keeping teams engaged during uncertainty, empowering employees, and guiding them through change with empathy and transparency. Additionally, we'll discuss the significance of building support networks and cultivating a resilient culture through effective leadership.

Recognizing the Role of Managers During Challenging Times

1. **Anchor of Stability**: Managers serve as the anchor of stability during adversity, providing guidance and reassurance to their

teams.

2. **Decision-Making**: They are tasked with making crucial decisions that can shape the organization's response to challenges.

3. **Team Morale**: Managers significantly impact team morale and motivation, influencing how teams weather challenging times.

4. **Communication Hub**: They act as the primary communication hub between senior leadership and front-line employees.

5. **Adaptability**: Managers must exemplify adaptability and resilience, setting an example for their teams.

Strategies for Remaining Calm and Composed Under Pressure

- **Mindfulness Practices**: Engaging in mindfulness techniques helps managers stay focused and composed amidst chaos.

- **Time Management**: Effective time management minimizes stress and ensures crucial tasks are addressed promptly.

- **Pause and Reflect**: Taking a moment to pause before reacting allows managers to respond thoughtfully rather than impulsively.

- **Delegating Responsibly**: Delegating tasks appropriately lightens the workload, preventing burnout and decision fatigue.

- **Stay Informed:** Staying informed about the situation is essential for making informed decisions and guiding teams effectively.

Case Study: Manager Navigating a Company-Wide Restructuring

In a recent company-wide restructuring, Sarah, a seasoned manager, demonstrated exceptional leadership:

- Clear Communication: Sarah communicated the changes transparently, addressing concerns and uncertainties head-on.

- Empathy: She understood the emotional impact and offered support to affected employees, displaying empathy and understanding.

- Involving the Team: Sarah involved her team in brainstorming solutions, empowering them to contribute to the reshaping process.

- Adaptable Leadership: She adapted her leadership style to provide extra guidance while allowing autonomy where appropriate.

- Staying Focused: Sarah remained focused on the organization's long-term goals, ensuring that decisions aligned with the company's mission.

Fostering Open Communication Channels During Crises

- Regular Updates: Maintain a rhythm of regular updates to keep the team informed about changes and progress.

- Two-Way Communication: Encourage open dialogue, inviting team members to share concerns and ideas.

- Active Listening: Listen actively to employee feedback, demonstrating that their opinions are valued.

- Accessibility: Make yourself accessible to team members who need support or have questions.

- Clear Expectations: Clearly outline roles, responsibilities, and expectations to prevent confusion.

Making Tough Decisions While Staying True to Values

- Values Alignment: Base decisions on the organization's core values, ensuring they remain intact despite challenges.
- Ethical Considerations: Consider the ethical implications of decisions on stakeholders and the broader community.
- Long-Term Impact: Evaluate decisions in the context of their long-term impact, avoiding short-sighted choices.
- Transparency: Communicate the rationale behind tough decisions transparently to maintain trust.
- Balancing Priorities: Balance the needs of the organization, employees, and stakeholders when making difficult choices.

Tips for Maintaining Team Engagement During Uncertainty

- Clear Direction: Provide a clear sense of direction even amid uncertainty, so the team knows where they are headed.
- Acknowledge Concerns: Acknowledge team members' concerns and address them empathetically.
- Celebrate Wins: Celebrate small victories to maintain morale and motivation during challenging periods.
- Professional Development: Offer opportunities for skill development and growth to show your investment in their futures.
- Regular Check-Ins: Conduct regular one-on-one check-ins to provide personalized support and guidance.

Empowering Employees to Contribute to Solutions

- Inclusive Problem-Solving: Encourage employees to contribute their insights and suggestions to tackle challenges collectively.

- Recognize Expertise: Acknowledge the expertise and strengths of individual team members, empowering them to lead in their areas.

- Ownership and Accountability: Give employees ownership of specific tasks, fostering a sense of responsibility and accountability.

- Support Innovation: Support and reward innovative ideas that can drive positive change within the organization.

- Feedback Loop: Establish a feedback loop to assess the effectiveness of implemented solutions and iterate as necessary.

Guiding Teams Through Change with Empathy and Transparency

- Emotional Intelligence: Employ emotional intelligence to understand and address the emotions that arise during change.

- Communication Cadence: Maintain a consistent communication cadence to keep the team informed about change progress.

- Acknowledge Discomfort: Acknowledge the discomfort of change while highlighting its potential for growth.

- Encourage Adaptability: Encourage team members to embrace change and adapt to new circumstances.

- Feedback Integration: Incorporate team feedback into the change process, making them feel heard and valued.

Building a Support Network Within and Outside the Organization

- Internal Network: Cultivate relationships within the organization to seek guidance, share experiences, and collaborate.

- Mentorship: Engage in mentorship relationships to gain insights from experienced peers and leaders.

- External Resources: Tap into external resources, such as industry associations and professional networks, for diverse perspectives.

- Peer Groups: Join peer groups or forums where managers facing similar challenges can share insights and strategies.

- Cross-Functional Collaboration: Collaborate with leaders from other departments to gain a holistic understanding of challenges.

Creating a Culture of Resilience Through Leadership

- Lead by Example: Demonstrate resilience in your own actions and decision-making to inspire your team.

- Learning from Setbacks: Use setbacks as opportunities for growth and learning, modeling a resilient mindset.

- Appreciation and Recognition: Recognize and celebrate team resilience, acknowledging their efforts during tough times.

- Continuous Improvement: Encourage a culture of continuous improvement, where challenges are viewed as stepping stones to progress.

- Shared Values: Reinforce shared values that prioritize adaptability and perseverance in the face of adversity.

As we navigate through the complexities of leadership during challenging times, it's essential to recognize the pivotal role managers play. By implementing strategies that maintain composure, foster open communication, and empower teams, leaders can not only steer their organizations through adversity but also cultivate a culture of resilience and growth. Through effective leadership, managers become the guiding light that propels their teams forward, even in the darkest of times.

Chapter 5

Building Resilient Teams

Building a resilient team is crucial for any organization's success, particularly in the nonprofit sector. In this chapter, we'll explore the significance of fostering resilience within a team, strategies for creating a psychologically safe work environment, a real-life case study of a nonprofit team overcoming funding challenges, and the importance of recognizing and valuing diverse perspectives. Additionally, we'll delve into techniques for promoting collaboration and cohesion, tips for developing cross-functional skills, leveraging strengths to tackle challenges, and encouraging continuous learning. We'll also provide guidelines for providing constructive feedback and growth opportunities, as well as nurturing a team culture that thrives in adversity.

Importance of Fostering Resilience in Your Team

Fostering resilience within a team is essential because it equips members to navigate challenges, setbacks, and uncertainties effectively. Resilient teams bounce back from failures, adapt to changing circumstances, and maintain their performance even under pressure.

Strategies for Creating a Psychologically Safe Work Environment

- Open Communication: Encourage open dialogue where team members can express their ideas, concerns, and feedback without fear of retribution.
- Active Listening: Promote active listening to ensure that everyone's perspectives are heard and valued.
- Non-Judgmental Attitude: Foster an environment where mistakes are seen as learning opportunities rather than failures.
- Empathy: Cultivate empathy among team members, enabling them to understand and support each other's challenges.
- Clear Expectations: Set clear expectations for behavior and communication norms, ensuring a respectful and inclusive environment.

Case Study: Non-Profit Team Overcoming Funding Challenges Together

In a non-profit organization facing severe funding challenges, the team demonstrated exceptional resilience by:

- Open Communication: The team shared the financial situation transparently, allowing members to collectively brainstorm solutions.

- Collaboration: They leveraged each member's strengths and skills to create a comprehensive fundraising strategy.
- Support System: The team provided emotional support, fostering a sense of unity and shared responsibility.
- Adaptive Leadership: Leaders encouraged innovative approaches and adaptive thinking to overcome obstacles.
- Continuous Learning: The experience prompted the team to acquire new skills and learn from the situation.

Recognizing and Valuing Diverse Perspectives Within the Team

- Inclusive Decision-Making: Involve team members from diverse backgrounds in decision-making to benefit from varied viewpoints.
- Cultural Sensitivity: Educate the team about different cultural perspectives and promote mutual respect.
- Diverse Teams: Form teams with diverse skill sets, backgrounds, and experiences to enrich problem-solving.
- Celebrating Differences: Create a culture where differences are celebrated, fostering creativity and innovation.
- Feedback Loop: Establish a feedback loop where team members can share their experiences and perspectives openly.

Techniques for Promoting Collaboration and Cohesion

- Team-building Activities: Organize team-building activities to strengthen interpersonal relationships and trust.
- Cross-Functional Projects: Assign cross-functional projects to encourage collaboration across different departments.
- Clear Goals: Set clear goals and roles for each team member to promote a shared sense of purpose.
- Regular Meetings: Conduct regular team meetings to discuss progress, challenges, and celebrate achievements.
- Feedback Culture: Develop a culture of constructive feedback that encourages open discussion and improvement.

Tips for Developing Cross-Functional Skills Among Team Members

- Skill Swapping: Encourage team members to share their skills with others, fostering a culture of continuous learning.
- Training Opportunities: Provide training and development opportunities that extend beyond individual roles.
- Job Rotation: Implement job rotation to give team members exposure to different functions within the organization.
- Skill-Sharing Sessions: Organize skill-sharing sessions where team members can teach each other new skills.
- Mentorship: Establish mentorship programs to facilitate the transfer of expertise between team members.

Leveraging Strengths and Talents to Tackle Challenges

- Strength Assessment: Identify individual strengths and talents within the team to assign tasks that align with these strengths.

- Collaborative Problem-Solving: Encourage team members to collaborate based on their strengths, leading to innovative solutions.

- Skill Synergy: Combine different strengths to create a complementary team dynamic that maximizes effectiveness.

- Appreciation and Acknowledgment: Regularly acknowledge and appreciate each team member's unique contributions.

- Goal-Oriented Assignments: Assign tasks that capitalize on the strengths of multiple team members to achieve common goals.

Encouraging Continuous Learning and Skill Development

- Learning Resources: Provide access to online courses, workshops, and industry conferences for skill enhancement.

- Learning Goals: Collaboratively set individual and team learning goals to foster a culture of continuous improvement.

- Knowledge Sharing: Encourage team members to share insights and newly acquired knowledge with the team.

- Learning Events: Organize lunch-and-learn sessions or webinars on relevant topics to facilitate skill development.

- Feedback for Growth: Provide constructive feedback and suggestions for skill improvement to promote development.

Guidelines for Providing Constructive Feedback and Growth Opportunities

- Timely Feedback: Provide feedback promptly after an event or task to ensure relevance and effectiveness.
- Specificity: Be specific about what was done well and areas that need improvement to guide growth.
- Constructive Tone: Frame feedback in a positive and constructive manner to encourage receptiveness.
- Two-Way Communication: Encourage team members to share their perspectives on feedback and contribute to improvement plans.
- Goal-Oriented: Align feedback with growth goals, emphasizing how improvements can benefit the individual and the team.

Nurturing a Team Culture That Thrives in Adversity

- Resilience as a Value: Make resilience a core value of the team, encouraging members to view challenges as opportunities.
- Adaptive Leadership: Leaders should model adaptability and resilience, setting an example for the team.
- Celebrating Resilience: Recognize and celebrate instances of resilience and innovative problem-solving within the team.
- Team Reflection: Periodically conduct team reflections on how challenges were overcome and lessons learned.
- Continuous Improvement: Incorporate lessons from challenges into team processes, creating a cycle of growth.

Building a resilient team is a multifaceted process that involves creating a safe and inclusive environment, fostering collaboration, recognizing diverse perspectives, and valuing continuous learning. By embracing these strategies and cultivating a culture of resilience, nonprofit organizations can build teams that thrive in adversity, adapt to change, and contribute to meaningful and lasting impact.

Chapter 6

Self-Care for Managers

In the dynamic and often demanding world of management, prioritizing self-care is not just a luxury but a necessity. As managers bear the weight of responsibilities and expectations, their well-being directly influences team performance and organizational success. This chapter delves into strategies for effective self-care, setting boundaries, recognizing signs of stress, and leading by example to promote well-being within teams. Drawing on case studies and practical advice, this chapter guides managers on maintaining balance, managing stress, and fostering a healthy work-life equilibrium.

Prioritizing Self-Care in a Demanding Managerial Role

In the whirlwind of managerial responsibilities, self-care can often take a backseat. However, it's crucial to recognize that taking care of oneself enhances one's ability to lead effectively. Managers must understand that self-care is not selfish; it's an investment in their own resilience and their team's success.

Strategies for Setting Healthy Boundaries and Managing Workload

Effective managers know the art of setting healthy boundaries to prevent burnout. Strategies include:

- **Clear Communication**: Communicate your availability and preferred contact times to manage expectations.
- **Delegate Wisely**: Empower your team by delegating tasks and responsibilities appropriately.
- **Learn to Say No**: Politely decline tasks that exceed your capacity, focusing on priorities.

Case Study: Manager Avoiding Burnout through Self-Care Practices

Meet Alex Turner, a dedicated and results-driven manager in a fast-paced technology company. As the head of a critical project team, Alex was constantly juggling deadlines, team dynamics, and organizational expectations. In the midst of his demanding role, he found himself on the brink of burnout. However, instead of succumbing to the pressure, Alex decided to take charge of his well-being through mindful self-care practices.

The Turning Point: Recognizing Burnout Signs

Alex's wake-up call came when he noticed persistent fatigue, irritability, and a decrease in his performance quality. He realized that his once-thriving enthusiasm had been replaced by a sense of overwhelm. Alarmed by the toll his workload was taking on his mental and physical health, he knew he needed a change.

Incorporating Self-Care: A Holistic Approach

Alex understood that self-care wasn't just about sporadic indulgences; it was a commitment to his well-being. He embarked on a journey of self-discovery and empowerment, integrating various practices into his daily routine:

- **Mindful Morning Rituals**: Alex started his mornings with meditation and visualization exercises. This routine allowed him to set positive intentions for the day ahead and cultivate a calm mindset.
- **Scheduled Breaks**: Realizing the value of breaks, Alex incorporated short moments of relaxation throughout his day. These brief pauses provided the mental clarity he needed to tackle challenges more effectively.
- **Physical Activity**: Recognizing the importance of physical health, Alex engaged in regular exercise. He began with brisk walks during lunch breaks, gradually increasing his physical activity.
- **Healthy Nutrition**: Alex shifted his focus to nourishing his body with nutritious meals. He minimized processed foods and sugary snacks, opting for balanced options that provided sustained

energy.

- **Tech Detox**: Aware of the negative impact of constant connectivity, Alex established "tech-free zones" during his evenings to disconnect from work-related emails and messages.

- **Hobbies Rekindled**: Alex revived his hobbies, particularly playing the guitar, which allowed him to channel his creative energy and find joy outside of work.

Results and Impact

Over time, Alex's commitment to self-care brought about transformative results:

- **Enhanced Resilience**: Alex's mindful practices equipped him with emotional resilience, enabling him to navigate challenges with a clear and focused mindset.

- **Improved Performance**: By prioritizing his well-being, Alex noticed an improvement in his performance quality. His ability to strategize and make critical decisions sharpened.

- **Strengthened Relationships**: The positive effects of self-care extended to his interactions with his team. Alex's improved emotional well-being positively influenced team dynamics and collaboration.

- **Burnout Averted**: Most importantly, Alex successfully averted burnout. He was no longer on the verge of exhaustion; he had transformed his approach to work and life.

Lessons Learned

Alex's journey holds valuable lessons for managers:

- **Self-Care is Non-Negotiable**: Prioritizing self-care isn't a luxury; it's an essential component of effective leadership and well-being.

- **Mindful Practices Work Wonders**: Mindfulness techniques such as meditation and visualization can significantly impact mental clarity and emotional balance.

- **Balance Breeds Success**: Striking a balance between work and personal life is crucial for sustainable success. Self-care supports this equilibrium.

- **Lead by Example**: Alex's commitment to self-care didn't go unnoticed by his team. His journey inspired them to adopt healthier habits and fostered a culture of well-being within the workplace.

- **It's an Ongoing Journey**: Self-care is a continuous journey, not a one-time fix. Regular practice yields long-term benefits.

Alex's case study illustrates that even in the most demanding managerial roles, burnout can be prevented through intentional self-care. By embracing mindfulness, physical well-being, and holistic practices, managers like Alex can not only sustain their performance but also inspire their teams to prioritize well-being. As a testament to the transformative power of self-care, Alex's story serves as a reminder that effective leadership starts with taking care of oneself.

Identifying Signs of Stress and Addressing Them Proactively

Stress is a common companion in managerial roles. Identifying signs such as fatigue, irritability, and sleep disturbances is crucial. Proactive steps include:

- Self-Reflection: Regularly assess your mood and energy levels to catch early signs of stress.
- Time Management: Plan your tasks realistically to avoid excessive pressure and last-minute rushes.
- Healthy Coping Strategies: Replace unhealthy coping mechanisms with exercises, hobbies, or social interactions.

Techniques for Managing Time and Avoiding Overcommitment

Time management skills are a manager's lifeline. Techniques to prevent overcommitment include:

- Prioritization: Identify high-impact tasks and allocate time to them before less critical duties.
- Time Blocking: Set aside dedicated time blocks for specific tasks, minimizing multitasking.
- Flexibility: Allow for unexpected tasks while maintaining focus on the day's priorities.

Tips for Practicing Mindfulness and Managing Stress

Mindfulness is a powerful tool for managers to navigate stress:

- Mindful Breathing: Incorporate deep breathing exercises to manage stress in challenging situations.
- Daily Reflection: Set aside a few minutes each day to reflect on

your achievements and areas for improvement.

- Present-Moment Focus: Practice being fully present during meetings and conversations, enhancing focus and connection.

Balancing Work, Personal Life, and Hobbies

Achieving a harmonious work-life balance requires deliberate effort:

- Set Boundaries: Clearly define "off" hours and avoid work-related activities during personal time.
- Schedule Personal Activities: Treat personal activities as non-negotiable appointments, just like work commitments.
- Unplug: Disconnect from work-related devices during personal time to recharge without distractions.

Incorporating Physical Activity and Healthy Habits into Your Routine

Physical well-being significantly impacts mental resilience:

- Regular Exercise: Incorporate physical activity into your routine to boost energy levels and reduce stress.
- Healthy Diet: Maintain a balanced diet rich in nutrients that fuel your body and mind.
- Adequate Sleep: Prioritize quality sleep to enhance cognitive function and overall well-being.

Guidelines for Seeking Support and Professional Development

Managers should never hesitate to seek support and growth

opportunities:

- Mentorship: Seek guidance from experienced mentors to navigate challenges effectively.
- Professional Development: Engage in training, workshops, and courses to enhance your managerial skills.
- Peer Networks: Connect with other managers to share experiences, learn from each other, and gain new perspectives.

Leading by Example to Promote Well-Being Within the Team

Managers play a pivotal role in fostering a culture of well-being within their teams:

- Open Dialogue: Encourage open conversations about stress, workload, and self-care within the team.
- Flexible Policies: Advocate for flexible work arrangements that empower team members to prioritize their well-being.
- Recognition and Appreciation: Acknowledge and appreciate team members' efforts, promoting a positive and supportive environment.

Self-care for managers is not a luxury but a strategic imperative. By implementing effective strategies, recognizing signs of stress, and leading by example, managers can foster their own well-being while positively influencing the productivity and morale of their teams. In a world where leadership demands resilience, self-care emerges as the foundation of effective management.

Chapter 7

Communication and Conflict Resolution

Effective communication and conflict resolution play pivotal roles in fostering resilience within organizations. In this chapter, we will delve into the significance of communication in promoting resilience, strategies to manage conflicts, real-world case studies, active listening techniques, addressing negative feedback constructively, facilitating open discussions, navigating difficult conversations, ensuring transparency, and building a culture of open communication and collaboration. By understanding these principles and practices, organizations can cultivate a strong foundation for teamwork, adaptability, and long-term success.

The Role of Effective Communication in Resilience

Effective communication is a linchpin in building organizational resilience, serving as the essential conduit through which ideas, information, and strategies flow. In the face of challenges, uncertainties, and rapidly changing landscapes, organizations that prioritize and master the art of communication are better equipped to weather storms and emerge stronger. This chapter delves into the pivotal role of effective communication in nurturing resilience within organizations and explores how communication strategies can enhance adaptability, collaboration, and overall organizational well-being.

Foundations of Resilience

Organizational resilience is the capacity to not only withstand adversity but to transform challenges into opportunities. It's the ability to flex, adapt, and learn from setbacks, ultimately emerging more robust and prepared for the future. Effective communication acts as the cornerstone of this resilience by establishing a network that interconnects teams, departments, and individuals.

Enhanced Adaptability

In a rapidly evolving world, the ability to adapt is vital. Effective communication enables organizations to disseminate information swiftly, keeping all stakeholders in the loop about changes, updates, and evolving strategies. When the lines of communication are open and transparent, team members are empowered to pivot and recalibrate their efforts as circumstances change.

Building Cohesion

Resilience often thrives in a collaborative environment. Effective communication nurtures a sense of unity and shared purpose among team members. Clear communication ensures that everyone understands the broader organizational goals, fostering a collective drive to overcome challenges together.

Crisis Management

When crises hit, communication can make or break an organization. Timely, accurate, and empathetic communication to all stakeholders—including employees, clients, partners, and the public—is vital for maintaining trust and confidence. Transparent communication during a crisis demonstrates accountability and a commitment to addressing the situation.

Navigating Uncertainty

Effective communication plays a crucial role in managing uncertainty. By openly acknowledging uncertainty, leaders can create a safe space for teams to voice concerns and collaborate on solutions. When employees are kept informed, they are less likely to succumb to fear and anxiety, and instead, focus on constructive problem-solving.

Communication Strategies for Resilience

- **Transparency:** Openness about challenges, goals, and decision-making processes fosters a culture of trust. Transparency encourages honesty, discourages rumors, and ensures that everyone is on the same page.
- **Consistent Messaging**: Consistency in messaging across different channels helps to avoid confusion and ensures that everyone receives the same accurate information.
- **Two-Way Communication**: Encouraging a two-way flow of information—where feedback, questions, and concerns are actively solicited and addressed—creates an environment where everyone feels heard and valued.

- **Clear Direction**: Providing clear guidance and instructions during uncertain times alleviates confusion and empowers employees to make informed decisions.

- **Empathy**: Demonstrating empathy through communication shows that leaders understand and care about the challenges team members may be facing. This creates a sense of unity and support.

- **Adaptability**: Employing various communication channels, such as emails, video conferences, and instant messaging, ensures that information reaches everyone, even if the team is working remotely.

- **Regular Updates**: Regularly updating teams about progress, changes, and milestones keeps everyone engaged and informed about the organization's journey.

- **Training**: Training employees in effective communication practices equips them with the skills to express themselves clearly and engage in meaningful conversations.

The Digital Advantage in Communication

The digital era has provided new avenues for communication that transcend geographical boundaries. Virtual communication tools, social media platforms, and collaborative software enable organizations to maintain consistent communication, even in remote or distributed work environments. Video conferencing, for instance, allows for face-to-face interaction, bridging the gap between physical distances and maintaining a sense of connection.

Cultivating a Resilience Mindset

Effective communication isn't just about transmitting information—it's about nurturing a mindset of resilience. Leaders who communicate with positivity and optimism, even in challenging times, inspire their teams to remain solution-oriented. By focusing on lessons learned, growth opportunities, and the organization's ability to adapt, leaders can shape the narrative of resilience.

In an ever-changing world, where disruptions are commonplace, organizational resilience is paramount. Effective communication stands as a beacon, guiding organizations through uncertainties and challenges. It empowers individuals, teams, and entire organizations to remain agile, cohesive, and adaptive. When nurtured and prioritized, effective communication not only ensures that everyone is on the same page but also creates an environment where resilience flourishes, making the organization stronger and more prepared for whatever the future holds.

Strategies for Managing Conflicts and Disagreements

- Early Intervention: Address conflicts as soon as they arise, preventing them from escalating into larger issues that may disrupt team dynamics.
- Active Mediation: Designate a neutral party to mediate conflicts, ensuring a fair and unbiased resolution process.
- Constructive Dialogue: Encourage involved parties to engage in open, respectful conversations to express their perspectives and explore solutions.
- Collaborative Problem-Solving: Approach conflicts as

opportunities for creative problem-solving, involving all relevant stakeholders in finding a mutually beneficial solution.

- Clear Expectations: Establish clear communication guidelines and conflict resolution procedures to prevent misunderstandings and facilitate timely interventions.

Case Study: Manager Navigating Team Conflicts to Maintain Productivity

In a high-pressure project, conflicts emerged among team members due to differing opinions on project direction. The manager utilized several strategies to resolve the conflicts and maintain productivity:

- Open Dialogue: The manager initiated one-on-one conversations with each team member to understand their viewpoints and concerns.

- Mediation: For conflicting parties, the manager facilitated a mediated conversation where both sides shared their perspectives under guided discussion.

- Shared Goals: The manager refocused the team on the project's shared goals, highlighting the importance of collaboration and emphasizing their collective success.

- Mutual Agreement: Through active listening and negotiation, the team reached a mutual agreement that integrated various perspectives into the project plan.

- Regular Check-Ins: The manager continued to schedule regular check-ins to monitor progress, address any lingering concerns, and provide ongoing support.

Active Listening Techniques for Understanding Team Concerns

- Maintain Eye Contact: Maintain eye contact to show attentiveness and respect during conversations.

- Avoid Interrupting: Let the speaker finish before responding to ensure that their perspective is fully understood.

- Paraphrasing: Repeat what you've understood in your own words to confirm your understanding and show that you value their input.

- Empathetic Responses: Respond with empathy and understanding, acknowledging the speaker's emotions and concerns.

- Ask Open-Ended Questions: Encourage elaboration by asking open-ended questions that prompt the speaker to share more details.

Tips for Addressing Negative Feedback Constructively

- Separate Behavior from Person: When addressing negative feedback, focus on the behavior or action, not the person's character.

- Be Specific: Provide specific examples of the behavior in question to ensure clarity and avoid ambiguity.

- Offer Solutions: Instead of dwelling on the problem, propose potential solutions to rectify the situation.

- Maintain Privacy: Address negative feedback in a private setting to avoid embarrassment or defensiveness.

- Focus on Improvement: Frame the conversation as an opportunity for growth and improvement, emphasizing the organization's commitment to development.

Techniques for Facilitating Open Discussions and Feedback Loops

- Regular Team Meetings: Schedule regular team meetings where team members can openly share updates, concerns, and feedback.

- Anonymous Feedback: Implement anonymous feedback mechanisms, such as suggestion boxes or digital surveys, to encourage honest input.

- Rotation of Facilitators: Rotate the role of meeting facilitator to ensure diverse perspectives are considered and heard.

- Encourage Diverse Voices: Create a safe space where all team members feel comfortable expressing their opinions, regardless of their hierarchical position.

- Reflect and Act: Acknowledge and address the feedback received during discussions, demonstrating a commitment to improvement.

Navigating Difficult Conversations with Empathy and Clarity

- Prepare in Advance: Anticipate potential challenges and concerns, and prepare talking points to address them effectively.

- Active Listening: Listen attentively to the other party's concerns before responding, showing empathy and understanding.

- Use "I" Statements: Frame your statements using "I" to express your perspective without making the other person defensive.

- Stay Calm and Respectful: Maintain a composed demeanor and use respectful language, even in emotionally charged conversations.

- Seek Common Ground: Identify common goals or areas of agreement to establish a foundation for productive dialogue.

Guidelines for Providing Regular Updates and Transparency

- Scheduled Updates: Establish a regular cadence for providing updates, whether through meetings, emails, or designated communication channels.
- Transparent Communication: Share both successes and challenges openly, building a culture of transparency and trust.
- Clear and Concise Messaging: Ensure that updates are clear, concise, and relevant, focusing on the most important information.
- Anticipate Questions: Address potential questions or concerns proactively to minimize confusion and speculation.
- Two-Way Communication: Encourage questions and feedback in response to updates, fostering an open dialogue.

Using Communication to Foster Trust and Resilience

- Consistent Messaging: Deliver consistent messages across all communication channels to build credibility and trust.
- Honesty and Authenticity: Be honest about challenges and setbacks, demonstrating authenticity and relatability.
- Feedback Incorporation: Show that feedback is valued by actively incorporating suggestions and ideas into decision-making.
- Recognition and Appreciation: Recognize team members' efforts and contributions, fostering a sense of belonging and

appreciation.

- Celebrate Milestones: Celebrate achievements and milestones collectively, reinforcing a sense of shared success.

Building a Culture of Open Communication and Collaboration

- Leadership Role Model: Leaders should exemplify open communication and collaboration, setting the tone for the entire organization.

- Encourage Questions: Create an environment where asking questions and seeking clarity is encouraged, regardless of hierarchy.

- Cross-Functional Collaboration: Foster collaboration across different departments or teams, encouraging diverse perspectives.

- Knowledge Sharing: Establish platforms for sharing knowledge, insights, and best practices across the organization.

- Continuous Improvement: Regularly review communication processes and strategies to identify areas for enhancement.

Effective communication and conflict resolution are essential for creating resilient organizations that can thrive amidst challenges. By embracing open dialogue, active listening, transparency, empathy, and collaborative problem-solving, organizations can navigate conflicts, build trust, and foster a culture of resilience and adaptability. These principles serve as the foundation for a harmonious and productive work environment that paves the way for long-term success and growth.

Chapter 8

Leveraging Innovation and Creativity

In today's dynamic and rapidly evolving landscape, embracing innovation and nurturing creativity have become critical for organizations to not only survive but thrive. In this chapter, we delve into the significance of innovation as a pathway to resilience. We explore strategies for fostering creative thinking within teams, using a real-life case study to illustrate effective leadership during disruption. Recognizing the potential of failure as a stepping stone to innovation is essential, as is mastering techniques for brainstorming and idea generation. We offer insights into creating an environment conducive to experimentation, nurturing a culture that embraces change, and providing guidelines for implementing new solutions. Ultimately, building resilience through a culture of adaptive creativity is key, as is striking the right balance between leading innovation and managing associated risks and rewards.

Embracing Innovation as a Pathway to Resilience

- **Innovation's Role in Resilience**: Innovation isn't just about introducing novel concepts; it's a strategy for building resilience. By embracing innovation, organizations become more adaptable to change, better equipped to navigate disruptions, and capable of finding creative solutions to emerging challenges.

- **Agility in Problem-Solving**: Innovative practices encourage organizations to adapt quickly to unforeseen circumstances, fostering a sense of agility in problem-solving.

- **Staying Ahead of the Curve**: Embracing innovation ensures that an organization remains ahead of industry trends, positioning it as a thought leader and an industry driver.

- **Embracing Failure as Learning**: Innovation necessitates experimentation, which means not all ideas will succeed. However, viewing failure as an opportunity to learn and iterate is a crucial aspect of fostering innovation.

- **Stimulating Growth**: Innovation opens new avenues for growth by uncovering untapped markets, enhancing existing products, and expanding service offerings.

Strategies for Encouraging Creative Thinking within the Team

- Encouraging Diverse Perspectives: Cultivate a diverse team with varied backgrounds and experiences to bring fresh perspectives to the table.

- Open Communication: Foster an environment where team members feel comfortable sharing their ideas without fear of criticism.

- Cross-Functional Collaboration: Encourage collaboration across departments to break down silos and promote interdisciplinary ideation.

- Time for Reflection: Allocate time for team members to step back from day-to-day tasks and reflect on innovative ideas.

- Rewarding Creativity: Recognize and reward innovative contributions, reinforcing the importance of creative thinking.

Case Study: Manager Leading a Team to Pivot and Adapt During Disruption

In the face of disruption, effective leadership is pivotal. Consider the case of Sarah, a project manager who successfully navigated her team through a challenging situation:

Sarah's Approach:

- Transparent Communication: Sarah maintained open communication channels, sharing the situation's gravity and potential impact with her team.

- Empowering Ownership: She empowered her team to brainstorm solutions and actively participate in decision-making.

- Fostering Collaboration: Recognizing that innovative ideas often arise through collaboration, Sarah organized brainstorming sessions to tap into collective creativity.

- Experimentation and Flexibility: Sarah encouraged her team to experiment with new approaches and adapt quickly based on feedback and results.

- Adaptive Leadership: Sarah demonstrated adaptive leadership by adjusting strategies based on changing circumstances, while ensuring the team felt supported.

Recognizing the Potential of Failure in Fostering Innovation

- Learning from Mistakes: Failure isn't an endpoint but a stepping stone to innovation. Organizations that embrace failure as a learning opportunity can refine their ideas and approaches.

- Cultivating Risk-Taking: A culture that accepts calculated risks encourages employees to explore uncharted territory and generate groundbreaking ideas.

- Iterative Improvement: Viewing failure as a part of an iterative process encourages teams to refine and iterate upon their ideas until they achieve success.

- Removing Stigma: Destigmatizing failure creates a safe space for employees to take risks and share their ideas without fear of negative repercussions.

- Promoting Accountability: Teams that acknowledge their failures and take ownership of their outcomes are more likely to develop innovative solutions.

Techniques for Brainstorming and Generating New Ideas

- Mind Mapping: Visualizing ideas through mind maps helps teams identify connections, leading to new and creative solutions.

- Reverse Brainstorming: Instead of generating ideas for a solution, teams brainstorm ways to create the problem. This innovative approach often yields unique insights.

- SCAMPER Technique: SCAMPER stands for Substitute, Combine, Adapt, Modify, Put to another use, Eliminate, and Reverse. It's a structured technique to spark creative ideas.

- Role Reversal: Encourage team members to step into different roles and perspectives, which can lead to unexpected and inventive viewpoints.

- Random Stimulus: Introduce random words, images, or concepts to stimulate unconventional thinking and generate novel ideas.

Tips for Creating an Environment that Supports Experimentation

- Risk-Tolerant Leadership: Leadership that embraces calculated risks sets the tone for the organization's attitude toward experimentation.

- Resource Allocation: Allocate resources and time for experimentation, emphasizing that failure is an acceptable outcome as long as lessons are learned.

- Safe Space: Establish a safe environment where employees feel comfortable sharing their experimental ideas without fearing negative consequences.

- Encourage Collaboration: Collaborative efforts can lead to innovative solutions as team members build upon each other's ideas.
- Learning Culture: Promote a culture of continuous learning, where experimentation and failure are seen as opportunities for growth.

Nurturing a Culture that Embraces Change and Exploration

- Lead by Example: Leaders who embrace change and exploration set the precedent for the entire organization.
- Encourage Curiosity: Reward and celebrate curiosity-driven exploration that leads to unexpected discoveries and innovation.
- Flexibility and Adaptability: Cultivate a flexible work environment that accommodates experimentation and adapts to emerging ideas.
- Continuous Learning Initiatives: Develop learning programs that encourage employees to explore new skills and stay updated on industry trends.
- Cross-Functional Exchanges: Encourage employees to collaborate across departments, facilitating the exchange of innovative ideas.

Guidelines for Implementing New Ideas and Solutions

- Pilot Testing: Test new ideas on a smaller scale before implementing them organization-wide. This allows for adjustments based on initial feedback.
- Clear Communication: Clearly communicate the rationale behind

new ideas, addressing potential concerns and showcasing the benefits.

- Feedback Loop: Establish a feedback loop to gather input from employees and stakeholders, making improvements based on their insights.

- Incremental Implementation: Implement new ideas in stages, allowing the organization to monitor progress and make adjustments along the way.

- Data-Driven Decision Making: Use data analytics to measure the impact of new solutions and adjust strategies based on quantifiable results.

Building Resilience through a Culture of Adaptive Creativity

- Adaptive Problem-Solving: A culture of adaptive creativity equips employees to find innovative solutions even in the face of unexpected challenges.

- Flexibility and Agility: Organizations that nurture adaptive creativity are more agile and better positioned to respond to changing circumstances.

- Embracing Change: A culture that encourages adaptation and experimentation prepares the organization to embrace change proactively.

- Iterative Improvement: Teams that practice adaptive creativity continually refine their strategies, learning from each iteration.

- Employee Empowerment: Empowering employees to contribute their creative ideas fosters a sense of ownership and resilience.

Leading Innovation while Balancing Risk and Reward

- Assessing Risk Tolerance: Evaluate the organization's risk appetite and identify areas where calculated risks can lead to innovation.

- Risk Management Strategies: Implement risk management strategies to mitigate potential negative impacts of new ideas.

- Rewarding Initiative: Reward and recognize employees who take calculated risks and contribute innovative ideas that drive positive outcomes.

- Measuring ROI: Assess the potential rewards of implementing new ideas against the associated risks to make informed decisions.

- Continuous Evaluation: Continuously evaluate the balance between risk and reward, adapting strategies based on changing circumstances.

Embracing innovation and nurturing creativity are integral to an organization's success and resilience. By fostering a culture that encourages experimentation, adaptive thinking, and calculated risk-taking, organizations can stay ahead of the curve, navigate disruptions effectively, and lead with innovative solutions. It's a dynamic journey that requires leadership, collaboration, and a commitment to learning from both successes and failures. As organizations leverage innovation as a strategic advantage, they cultivate an environment where creativity flourishes, enabling them to thrive in an ever-changing world.

Chapter 9

Developing Long-Term Resilience

In a world that is constantly evolving, the key to success and fulfillment lies in the ability to adapt, learn, and grow. Developing long-term resilience is not just about surviving change, but thriving in the face of it. This chapter explores the mindset, strategies, and practices that enable individuals to cultivate resilience, continually improve themselves, and embrace change as a catalyst for growth.

Cultivating a Mindset of Lifelong Learning and Growth

Embracing a mindset of lifelong learning is the foundation of resilience. It involves recognizing that every experience, whether positive or challenging, holds an opportunity for growth. This mindset shifts the focus from perfection to progress, enabling individuals to:

- Embrace Challenges: Instead of shying away from challenges, a growth mindset encourages individuals to view them as chances to learn and improve.

- Learn from Failures: Failures are seen as stepping stones toward success, providing valuable insights and lessons for future endeavors.

- Seek Feedback: Constructive feedback is welcomed as a tool for self-improvement rather than a criticism of one's abilities.

- Persist in the Face of Obstacles: A growth mindset fosters resilience, allowing individuals to persist even when faced with setbacks.

Strategies for Continually Building Personal and Professional Skills

To remain resilient in an ever-changing world, individuals must continually build and refine their skills. This involves proactive steps such as:

- Continuous Education: Participate in workshops, courses, and seminars to stay updated with the latest knowledge and trends in your field.

- Skill Diversification: Expand your skill set to remain versatile and adaptable to different roles and responsibilities.

- Skill Deepening: Continually refine your existing skills to achieve mastery and stay relevant.

- Self-Assessment: Regularly assess your strengths and areas for improvement to tailor your learning efforts effectively.

Case Study: Manager's Journey of Continuous Self-Improvement

Consider the journey of a manager who exemplified the principles of continuous self-improvement. This manager:

- Pursued Education: Enrolled in online courses and attended industry conferences to stay current in a rapidly evolving field.

- Sought Mentorship: Sought guidance from seasoned professionals to learn from their experiences and gain insights.

- Adapted to Feedback: Embraced constructive feedback, using it to refine leadership skills and enhance team dynamics.

- Navigated Challenges: When faced with unexpected challenges, this manager approached them as opportunities to innovate and grow.

Techniques for Staying Adaptable in a Rapidly Changing World

Adaptability is a cornerstone of resilience, enabling individuals to thrive despite uncertainty. Techniques to enhance adaptability include:

- Cultivate Curiosity: Curiosity drives exploration and learning, enabling individuals to embrace new ideas and approaches.

- Practice Flexibility: Be open to changing plans and strategies when circumstances evolve.

- Focus on Problem-Solving: Approach challenges as puzzles to solve, using creativity and innovation to find solutions.

- Stay Open-Minded: Be receptive to different viewpoints, as they can lead to fresh insights and perspectives.

Tips for Seeking Out New Challenges and Opportunities

Seeking out new challenges and opportunities can stretch your abilities and contribute to your growth. Consider these tips:

- Step Outside Your Comfort Zone: Challenge yourself to undertake tasks or projects that are slightly beyond your current capabilities.
- Set Stretch Goals: Set goals that are ambitious but achievable, motivating you to push your limits.
- Volunteer for Projects: Offer to participate in projects that align with your interests and expose you to new experiences.
- Network Intentionally: Connect with individuals from diverse backgrounds and industries to gain fresh insights.

Navigating Career Transitions with Resilience and Confidence

Career transitions are opportunities for growth, yet they can be daunting. To navigate them with resilience:

- Reflect on Skills: Evaluate your transferable skills and strengths to identify how they can be applied in a new role or industry.
- Leverage Networking: Reach out to your professional network for advice, guidance, and potential opportunities.
- Embrace a Learning Mindset: Approach career transitions as learning experiences, acknowledging that there will be a learning curve.
- Build on Past Experiences: Draw from your previous experiences

to inform your decisions and strategies in your new role.

Guidelines for Setting Ambitious yet Achievable Goals

Setting goals that stretch your capabilities while remaining attainable is crucial for growth. Consider these guidelines:

- Specificity: Clearly define your goals, outlining the desired outcomes and the steps required to achieve them.
- Measurability: Set benchmarks to track your progress and measure your success.
- Realistic Ambition: Aim high, but ensure that your goals are realistic within the given time frame and resources.
- Adaptability: Be open to adjusting your goals based on changing circumstances and new information.

Maintaining a Support Network for Ongoing Development

Building resilience is not a solitary journey. A support network can provide encouragement, guidance, and motivation:

- Mentorship: Seek mentors who can offer insights, advice, and a broader perspective on your growth journey.
- Peer Relationships: Connect with peers who share similar aspirations, creating a sense of camaraderie and accountability.
- Accountability Partners: Partner with someone who holds you accountable for your goals and progress.
- Constructive Feedback: Surround yourself with individuals who provide honest and constructive feedback to aid your

development.

Building Resilience Through a Commitment to Improvement

Resilience is not solely a product of external factors; it also stems from an internal commitment to growth:

- Mindful Self-Reflection: Regularly reflect on your journey, acknowledging your achievements and identifying areas for improvement.
- Embrace Setbacks as Opportunities: Instead of dwelling on failures, view them as chances to learn and come back stronger.
- Practice Self-Compassion: Treat yourself with kindness and understanding, recognizing that growth is a gradual process.
- Cultivate Positive Habits: Establish routines that promote well-being, mental clarity, and emotional balance.

Embracing Change and Uncertainty as Catalysts for Growth

Change and uncertainty are inevitable aspects of life, and embracing them can lead to profound growth:

- Adopt a Positive Perspective: Reframe challenges as opportunities for growth and personal development.
- Focus on the Present: Cultivate mindfulness by grounding yourself in the present moment, reducing anxiety about the future.
- View Change as a Learning Opportunity: Approach change with curiosity, seeking to learn from new experiences and situations.
- Build Resilience Muscles: Every challenge and change you

navigate enhances your resilience muscles, preparing you for future endeavors.

In a world that is in a constant state of flux, developing long-term resilience is not just a choice; it is a necessity. By cultivating a growth mindset, honing your skills, embracing change, and seeking out new opportunities, you can not only navigate the uncertainties of life but also flourish in the process. Remember, the journey of resilience is a continuous one, marked by self-improvement, adaptability, and an unwavering commitment to growth.

Chapter 10

The Resilient Manager's Legacy

In the journey of leadership, the concept of resilience stands as a guiding force, shaping the paths managers traverse and the impact they leave behind. This chapter delves into the legacy of a resilient manager, exploring strategies to pass on resilience skills, case studies highlighting the manager's impact, and the lasting effects of a resilient leadership style. Techniques for imprinting positivity, mentoring, guiding teams toward resilience, fostering adaptability, and embracing one's legacy are all part of the resilient manager's enduring impact.

Reflecting on the Journey of Resilience as a Manager

- Defining Resilience: For a manager, resilience goes beyond mere survival; it's the ability to lead effectively amidst challenges, adapt to change, and inspire teams to persevere.

- Lessons from Setbacks: Reflecting on personal setbacks and how they were navigated provides insights that foster resilience in managers. The ability to learn from failures strengthens their leadership.

- Adapting to Change: Resilience isn't just about surviving change; it's about thriving in it. Managers who model adaptability teach teams to embrace uncertainty.

- Staying Committed: Resilient managers remain committed to their vision despite obstacles. This unwavering dedication becomes a beacon for their teams.

- Inspiring Amidst Adversity: Resilience in leadership is showcased when managers uplift their teams during tough times, demonstrating emotional fortitude.

Strategies for Passing on Resilience Skills to Future Leaders

- Lead by Example: Managers must embody resilience themselves, showcasing how to navigate challenges and maintain a positive outlook.

- Open Communication: Encouraging open conversations about setbacks and lessons learned instills a culture of resilience within the team.

- Training and Workshops: Organize training sessions that focus on developing resilience skills, providing practical tools to handle stress and adversity.

- Mentorship Programs: Pair experienced resilient managers with emerging leaders, allowing them to learn firsthand how to overcome obstacles.

- Goal Setting: Teach the art of setting realistic goals and maintaining focus, even in the face of setbacks.

Case Study: Manager's Impact on Team Members' Resilience

In a software company, Manager A faced a project delay due to unforeseen technical issues. Instead of panicking, Manager A gathered the team, discussed potential solutions, and emphasized the importance of collective problem-solving. This approach bolstered the team's morale and problem-solving skills. As a result, the project was successfully completed, and team members learned the value of resilience and adaptability.

Identifying the Lasting Effects of a Resilient Leadership Style

- Team Empowerment: Resilient leaders empower their teams, encouraging them to take initiative and ownership in overcoming challenges.

- Positive Organizational Culture: A resilient leadership style contributes to a positive workplace culture where employees feel supported and motivated.

- Long-Term Success: Teams led by resilient managers are more likely to achieve long-term success by navigating adversity effectively.

- Skill Development: Resilient leaders foster skill development, as team members learn problem-solving, adaptability, and resourcefulness.

- Employee Retention: A culture of resilience enhances employee retention, as individuals are more likely to stay in an environment that values their growth.

Techniques for Leaving a Positive Imprint on Your Team and Organization

- Appreciation and Recognition: Regularly acknowledge team efforts and individual contributions to boost morale and create a positive atmosphere.

- Constructive Feedback: Provide feedback that highlights strengths while suggesting areas for improvement, fostering growth-oriented mindsets.

- Emotional Intelligence: Show empathy and emotional intelligence, creating a supportive environment where team members feel understood.

- Collaborative Decision-Making: Involve the team in decision-making processes, fostering a sense of ownership and camaraderie.

- Development Opportunities: Offer learning and development opportunities that contribute to personal and professional growth.

Tips for Mentoring and Inspiring the Next Generation of Managers

- Individualized Guidance: Tailor mentoring to each individual's strengths, weaknesses, and aspirations, providing personalized support.

- Encourage Experimentation: Urge emerging managers to step out of their comfort zones, embrace new challenges, and learn from failures.

- Promote Lifelong Learning: Instill a passion for continuous learning, emphasizing that growth and development never cease.

- Lead through Stories: Share personal anecdotes of resilience and growth, illustrating how challenges can be transformative.

- Balanced Work-Life Integration: Highlight the importance of balancing work and personal life to maintain well-being and sustain resilience.

Guiding Teams to Embrace Resilience as a Core Value

- Resilience as a Mindset: Encourage teams to view challenges as opportunities for growth and learning, shifting their mindset toward resilience.

- Cultivate Support Networks: Foster an environment where team members support each other through tough times, creating a sense of unity.

- Celebrate Efforts: Recognize and celebrate team efforts, even if outcomes aren't always as expected. Acknowledging progress boosts morale.

- Learning from Failure: After setbacks, facilitate discussions that focus on lessons learned, promoting a culture of continuous improvement.
- Resourcefulness: Teach teams to maximize available resources and find innovative solutions to problems.

Fostering a Culture of Adaptability and Growth

- Embrace Change: Demonstrate openness to change and adaptability, signaling to the team that change is a natural part of growth.
- Feedback Culture: Create an environment where feedback is welcomed and used to drive positive change.
- Agile Decision-Making: Encourage quick, informed decision-making in response to evolving circumstances.
- Continuous Improvement: Promote the idea that there's always room for improvement, both individually and as a team.
- Learning from Success: Analyze successful projects to identify patterns that can be replicated in future endeavors.

Recognizing That Resilience Is an Ongoing Journey

- Continuous Learning: Stress that resilience is not a destination but a journey that requires ongoing learning and adaptation.
- Reflect and Adapt: Encourage individuals to periodically reflect on their resilience strategies and make necessary adjustments.
- Seeking Support: Remind managers and teams that seeking support from mentors, peers, or counselors is a sign of strength, not weakness.

- Growth Mindset: Cultivate a growth mindset where challenges are embraced as opportunities to learn and develop.
- Adapt to Context: Recognize that different situations may require different approaches to resilience, and flexibility is key.

Embracing the Legacy of a Resilient and Impactful Manager

- Lead with Purpose: Reflect on the impact you wish to leave behind and ensure your actions align with that purpose.
- Document Success Stories: Create a repository of success stories that showcase how your leadership positively affected individuals and projects.
- Sustain Relationships: Stay connected with past team members and colleagues, maintaining a network that can continue to benefit from your wisdom.
- Offer Guidance: Even after moving on, remain available to provide guidance and insights to those you've mentored.
- Celebrate Achievements: Celebrate the milestones achieved by your teams and individuals, highlighting the lasting effects of your leadership.

In closing, the legacy of a resilient manager is one of enduring impact. Through fostering resilience in oneself and others, imparting skills, and shaping organizational cultures, these managers leave behind a legacy that resonates long after they've moved on. By embracing the journey of resilience, they guide the future generation of leaders and contribute to the growth and success of their teams and organizations.

The Resilient Manager: How to Bounce Back from Setbacks and Thrive in Adversity" offers a comprehensive guide to developing the essential skills and mindset required to navigate the ever-evolving landscape of leadership. Through the exploration of real-world case studies, practical tips, and actionable guidelines, this book empowers managers to overcome challenges with grace, adaptability, and determination. By mastering the art of resilience, leaders can not only weather storms but also inspire their teams and organizations to rise above difficulties. The journey to becoming a resilient manager is a transformative one, leading to enhanced leadership effectiveness, greater personal growth, and a lasting positive impact. Whether you're an aspiring leader or an experienced manager seeking to enhance your leadership abilities, "The Resilient Manager" equips you with the tools needed to bounce back from setbacks and thrive in the face of adversity.

Key Takeaways

1. **Resilience as a Leadership Skill**: Learn to cultivate resilience as a fundamental leadership skill, allowing you to face challenges head-on and inspire your team to do the same.

2. **Adapting to Change**: Understand that change is inevitable and develop the ability to adapt to new situations, technologies, and market dynamics.

3. **Managing Setbacks**: Embrace setbacks as opportunities for growth. Discover strategies to handle failures, setbacks, and crises in a constructive manner.

4. Emotional Intelligence: Enhance your emotional intelligence to effectively manage stress, stay composed during challenging times, and maintain strong relationships with your team.

5. **Decision-Making Under Pressure**: Develop a resilient decision-making process that thrives under pressure. Learn to evaluate options, make sound judgments, and communicate effectively.

6. **Maintaining Team Morale**: Discover techniques to maintain team morale and motivation during difficult times. Lead by example and provide a supportive environment.

7. **Leading by Example**: Showcase resilience through your actions. Set an example for your team, fostering a culture of perseverance and adaptability.

8. **Self-Care and Well-being**: Prioritize self-care to sustain your energy levels and overall well-being. Explore techniques for managing stress, maintaining work-life balance, and avoiding burnout.

9. **Effective Communication**: Hone your communication skills to convey your vision, goals, and strategies clearly, especially during times of uncertainty.

10. **Continuous Learning**: Embrace a mindset of continuous learning and growth. Regularly seek feedback, reflect on experiences, and seek opportunities for professional development.

11. **Inspiring Others**: Inspire and mentor your team to cultivate resilience. Empower them with the tools to navigate challenges and foster a resilient organizational culture.

12. **Strategic Planning**: Develop a strategic approach to managing adversity. Create contingency plans and assess risks to ensure your team is prepared for various scenarios.

13. **Case Studies and Real-Life Examples**: Draw inspiration from real-world case studies and examples of successful leaders who demonstrated resilience in challenging situations.

14. **Guidelines for Non-Profit Leadership**: Explore insights specific to non-profit organizations, including fundraising challenges, stakeholder management, and navigating social impact.

15. **Balancing Empathy and Decision-Making**: Find the balance between being empathetic towards your team's concerns and making tough decisions for the organization's benefit.

"The Resilient Manager" equips you with a holistic toolkit for developing and strengthening your resilience as a manager. By internalizing these takeaways, you'll be prepared to face adversity, guide your team through challenges, and lead with confidence, ensuring both personal and organizational growth.

About the Author

Iqbal Shah is a multifaceted individual driven by his passions for writing, blogging, and graphic design. With over two decades of experience in the non-profit sector, he brings a wealth of knowledge and expertise to his endeavors. As a dedicated blogger, Iqbal shares his insights on subjects close to his heart, fueled by his genuine interest in various topics.

Not only a wordsmith, but Iqbal also possesses a creative flair as a graphic designer. His talent shines through in the captivating visuals he designs, which often accompany his written work. Combining his skills in writing and graphic design, Iqbal crafts unique and engaging content that leaves a lasting impact on his readers.

Throughout his career in the non-profit sector, Iqbal has demonstrated a strong commitment to making a positive difference in the lives of others. His passion for social causes drives his work, inspiring both his writing and design projects to carry meaningful messages and advocate for change.

In his spare time, Iqbal can be found immersing himself in new creative endeavors, always eager to explore and expand his skillset. His dedication to continuous learning and personal growth ensures that he remains at the forefront of his craft, consistently producing high-quality work.

Through his diverse talents and unwavering passion, Iqbal continues to make a significant impact in both the creative and non-profit realms. With each project he takes on, he strives to leave a positive mark on the world, making him an inspiring and humble force in his chosen fields.

www.ingramcontent.com/pod-product-compliance
Lightning Source LLC
Chambersburg PA
CBHW062343290526
45794CB00005B/2089